AF657260

Migration and Women Casual Workers

A Study in Superexploitation

Migration and Women Casual Workers

A Study in Superexploitation

Shankar Gopalakrishnan, Anita Juneja,
Trepan Singh Chauhan, Ramendra Kumar
and M.S. Selvaraj

KISLAY Social Research Collective

AAKAR

Migration and Women Casual Workers: A Study in Superexploitation
Shankar Gopalakrishnan, Anita Juneja, Trepan Singh Chauhan, Ramendra Kumar and M.S. Selvaraj

First Published 2018

ISBN 978-93-5002-591-8

Any part or whole of this document may be reproduced for non-commercial purposes provided due credited is given to the authors and the publisher.

Published by
AAKAR BOOKS
28 E Pocket IV, Mayur Vihar Phase I
Delhi 110 091 India
aakarbooks@gmail.com

Laser Typeset at
Sakshi Computers, Delhi

Printed at
D.K. Fine Art Press, Delhi

Contents

1

Introduction

Migration is now a central part of India's socioeconomic landscape, but few of the studies and policy discussions on this issue address the reality that the majority of migrants in India are women. In 2007-08, for instance, the NSSO found that 48 per cent of women residents in rural areas and 46 per cent in urban areas were migrants—as compared to 6 per cent and 26 per cent for men (National Sample Survey Organisation 2010). Yet this fact remains almost entirely invisible in discussions around migration, and particularly when discussing migrant workers. In this study, we aim to examine the experiences and living conditions of migrant women workers, and in particular workers of a particular type—inter-state migrant women who work as casual or daily wage workers, or who belong to families dependent on such labour, at their site of destination. Drawing on field surveys from three states—Uttarakhand, Tamil Nadu and Delhi—we felt that this study may help address three shortcomings in the existing literature.

First, existing studies on women migrant workers often rely either on official data at the macro level (see, for instance, Shanthi (2006) or Bhatt (2009)), or on large-scale field surveys such as that reported in Mazumdar (2013), which covered thousands of households across the country. These studies offer crucial insights into the changing shape of migration overall, but they do not have the scope to look at specific dynamics, and especially at the relationship between women and men within families that result from this form of migration.

Second, migrants for casual labour experience a specific form of oppression that is particularly easy to miss in large-scale studies that look across occupational categories. Indeed, migrant casual and daily wage workers are among the most superexploited segments of Indian society, subjected to a combination of caste, class, patriarchal and community-based systems of oppression. While workers who are trafficked, who work in brick kilns, sugarcane, sex work or other highly exploitative industries face more brutal forms of exploitation, the number of casual and daily wage workers is likely far higher than these categories—and being ostensibly 'free' workers, their exploitation is elided both by discussions that focus only on particular sectors and by broad discussions that treat all migrants as a single category.

Finally, not all studies rely on macro data alone, of course Srinivasan (1997) provides a particularly evocative ethnographic study of a particular migration flow—in that case between two villages in Tamil Nadu and a slum in Delhi. Jan Breman's work, which looked at women, men and children, was a similarly sophisticated analysis of unorganised sector migration based on studies of a set of linked flows in Gujarat (for instance, Breman (1994)). These studies can draw out the exploitation and conditions under which particular groups of migrants live and work, and provide a useful complement to the macro-level studies. But they in turn may miss patterns that occur outside individual sites and migrant flows.

In this study, we have sought to, in one sense, address the gap between the ethnographic and macro-level studies by attempting a small-scale analysis that is nevertheless comparative across contexts and areas. We hope that by doing so we may be able to highlight structural features that may otherwise not be apparent—lost either in the specificity of ethnography or the broad-stroke nature of macro studies. We believe that a study of this nature may contribute to a wider discussion that is necessary in the current Indian political and economic context.

As a final note, this study builds on a prior study we completed in 2017—see Gopalakrishnan et al. (2017)—that predominantly looked at male daily wage workers in the same sites of destination. This study complements that earlier study, and is part of a three study series that will culminate in 2019 with a study examining the conditions and impact of migration on children. We hope this will provide a more complete and holistic picture of the political and social economy of migration in India.

Methodology

Our research study here draws upon two sets of information: secondary sources, primarily in the form of earlier studies and official data, and a field survey that was conducted in the states of Uttarakhand, Tamil Nadu and Delhi. The survey focused on workers living in the urban slums of Dehradun, in the areas near the city of Coimbatore and the Nilgiris district in Tamil Nadu, and in the urban slums of Delhi (in this sense it should be noted that we did not examine migration flows that terminate in rural areas). Our field surveys covered 100 workers in Tamil Nadu, 98 in Delhi and 60 in Dehradun.

Our general research focus, in this and other studies, has been on capturing qualitative experiences and placing them in a comparative framework. In light of this, and in view of our limited capacity, we did not seek or use a random or stratified sampling method. Our surveys instead followed a 'snowball' methodology to identify individual interviewees, and then combined this with group discussions and with the ground experience of the researchers (all of whom are familiar with these areas through other work[1]). In the context of this methodology, rigorous statistical conclusions should not be drawn from our data, and we have endeavoured to avoid doing so in this report as well.

Our study sample had the following characteristics. As noted earlier, all those interviewed were either themselves in casual labour or in contract labour that was very similar to casual labour in character. All these women also belonged to families that depended on such forms of labour for their survival. Within this overall focus, all three samples were predominantly from oppressed communities. Dalits formed 48 per cent of the sample in Dehradun, 33 per cent in Tamil Nadu and fully 90 per cent in Delhi (Adivasis were largely absent in the Delhi sample—only 3 per cent of those interviewed—while forming 41 per cent of those interviewed in Tamil Nadu and 10 per cent in Dehradun). Only 7 per cent of those interviewed in Dehradun, none in Tamil Nadu and 3 per cent of those in Delhi belonged to non-backward castes (the remainder of the sample belonged to the OBC and MBC communities). In religious terms, all three samples were predominantly Hindu—67 per cent in Dehradun, 73 per cent in Tamil Nadu and 94 per cent in Delhi. Muslims were significantly represented in Dehradun, forming 33 per cent of the sample, but were less represented in Delhi and Tamil Nadu (5 per cent and 3 per cent respectively). Only in Tamil Nadu was there a significant Christian presence (24 per cent). In all three samples, women from Bihar were a significant proportion of interviewees—17 per cent in Delhi, 19 per cent in Tamil Nadu and 30 per cent in Dehradun. The remaining source states varied depending on the site of destination—Delhi had its largest proportion from Madhya Pradesh (47 per cent) followed by Uttar Pradesh (24 per cent); while Dehradun had, unsurprisingly, a very high share from Uttar Pradesh (63 per cent). Tamil Nadu had the most varied geographical profile, with migrants from Chhattisgarh (22 per cent), Jharkhand (23 per cent), West Bengal (20 per cent), Odisha (10 per cent) and Andhra Pradesh (6 per cent) in our sample.

This community profile broadly matches both data and anecdotal impressions which confirm that daily wage and casual labour is predominantly performed by oppressed communities from poorer states. This then also correlates with the educational levels of those interviewed. In Dehradun 65 per cent of those interviewed were illiterate and only 8 per cent had studied up to the 9th Standard or higher. In Delhi, similarly, 70 per cent were illiterate and only 15 per cent had studied to over the 9th Standard (of which only 2 per cent had completed the 11th or 12th Standard, and none had studied at higher levels). In Tamil Nadu, approximately 10 per cent had completed the 9th Standard or higher, but a much lower proportion was illiterate—only 26 per cent, with the majority, 52 per cent, having studied between Classes 1 and 5.

In age terms, in Dehradun and Delhi, our sample included women ranging in age from 18 to 50, and in both cases 50 per cent fell between 23 and 30 years of age. In Tamil Nadu, the sample was significantly younger—71 per cent were between the ages of 16 and 22. This was also reflected in the marriage profiles of those interviewed. In both Dehradun and Delhi, the sample was essentially all married women (98 per cent and 95 per cent respectively), while in Tamil Nadu only 74 per cent were married.

There is one other area in which our samples differ from each other—the specific form of work the women were engaged in. In Dehradun 95 per cent of those interviewed were domestic workers, but 13 per cent also reported working in construction (women were able to report multiple forms of work if they engaged in them—see next section). In Delhi, these were also the two largest sectors by far, but the balance was different—66 per cent were in construction and only 21 per cent in domestic work. It should also be noted that in Delhi the survey process included a large number of women working, and living, on road sites. In Tamil Nadu, meanwhile, none of those interviewed was a domestic worker—25 per cent worked in construction and road work, 30 per cent on plantations, 36 per cent as contract/casual labour in factories and 9 per cent in other forms of work.

While these differences are primarily an artifact of our sampling methodology, it should be noted that they are not out of line with broader conditions in these sites. Women construction workers are, for instance, considerably rarer in Dehradun than in Delhi—perhaps reflecting a higher demand and a lower supply of migrants engaged in domestic work in Dehradun (see Kumar and Chauhan (2014) for a longer discussion on the comparative domestic work situation in the two cities). Similarly, in Tamil Nadu, inter-state migrants are far less likely to speak the local language, and hence far less likely to be employed in domestic situations.

A further discussion on the differences in the character of our samples, and the implications for our analysis, can be found in the penultimate section of this paper. However, before continuing, we should note one crucial limitation of our study—especially as compared to the previously-noted ethnographic studies discussed here. While all our interview teams were either primarily or solely composed of women, we did not seek extended, private discussions between women interviewees and women researchers in the manner that most ethnographic studies do, as this would have been out of the scope of a study of this nature (though a small proportion of those interviewed in all three sites already had a relationship of trust with the researchers as a result of other work). We endeavour to keep this limitation in mind below, and in this sense this report should be seen as only an initial exploration of these issues.

Background: The Scope of Women's Migration

In our previous 2017 study, we examined some of the driving 'push' and 'pull' factors behind daily wage and casual labour migration. Some of the factors we identified included the collapse of the agricultural sector, the increasing lack of viability of 'middle' class positions in rural areas,[2] and changing structures of employment and labour in rural areas.

Our sample among women workers also confirmed the roles of these factors in the particular migration flows we examined for this study. A significant proportion of those we interviewed—63 per cent of those interviewed in Delhi, 58 per cent in Dehradun and 21 per cent in Tamil Nadu—owned land in their home areas (the deviation in Tamil Nadu will be discussed further in the last section). These holdings were not necessarily very small. In the case of Dehradun and Delhi, 50 per cent and 60 per cent respectively of those interviewed possessed more than a bigha of land, and in Delhi 20 per cent of those interviewed owned seven or more bighas. In Tamil Nadu, we used the 'acre' measurement since that is the common unit there, and here too half of those holding land—11 per cent of the overall sample—reported owning two or more acres of land. All this indicates that our samples, except possibly in the case of some Tamil Nadu interviewees, did not arise from populations that were at the absolute extreme of rural poverty. Yet nevertheless they migrated and undertook casual labour in their destination sites, a testimony to the fact that official discourses on how only those in dire poverty migrate (or are subjected to the resulting vulnerability) are incorrect.

Indeed, the sheer unviability of much of the agricultural economy then becomes apparent when we look at how migrants responded to questions on economic conditions in their home areas. In both Dehradun and Delhi, only 35 per cent and 36 per cent of those interviewed reported any income at all from cultivation in their home areas (on rented or own land). In Tamil Nadu this proportion was higher—76 per cent—but the income reported was very low (less than Rs. 2,000 per month). A significant proportion of those interviewed reported incomes from wage labour in their home areas—47 per cent in Dehradun, 54 per cent in Delhi and 86 per cent in Tamil Nadu. This matches with reports of an overall shift in rural incomes towards an increased dependence on wage labour in general,[3] and confirms that our sample reflected populations who are neither completely destitute nor from richer or 'upper' classes in rural areas.

This question in turn is connected to one of the most vexed questions around the migration of women in India. Official data has shown a sharp increase in migration of women over the past three decades. According to the official figures, the reason for this is a steep rise in the number of women indicating that they migrated for purposes of marriage. For instance, NSSO data shows that the proportion of migrants "for purposes of marriage" among rural women jumped from 24.7 per cent in 1993 to 43.5 per cent in 2007-08 (Mazumdar 2013). Indeed, in 2007-08, the NSSO found that 91 per cent of rural female migrants and 61 per cent of urban female migrants reported marriage as the reason for their migration (National Sample Survey Organisation 2010).

This in turn has given rise to a heated debate about whether this reading is in fact correct, given that official surveys suffer from the limitation of only allowing women to state one reason for migrating. It has been commonly noted that migrating "for marriage" may disguise more economic reasons for migration, or the tendency of families to take into account the prospects of employment of both partners both when searching for partners and after marriage. For instance, Shanthi (2006) points out that the labour force participation rate for migrants, both women and men, shows sharp increases after migration; and all states, at least till 2000, showed steady increases in the number of "never married" women migrating for economic purposes. There has also been a shift, she argues, away from "male-selective migration" where men move first and women follow, towards women and men migrating together. But these arguments are questioned by other researchers—see for instance, Mazumdar (2013)—who argue that even if much female migration is 'disguised' economic migration, there is also a rise in marriages over long distances for other reasons, including the rise in dowry demands in all communities, falling sex ratios and a greater focus on village exogamy.

These debates are important for understanding the picture of women's migration decisions as a whole, but they can only be answered by better and more fine-grained macro-level data. Given the limitations in both the nature and size of our samples, we cannot shed much light on these larger debates here. However, the debates do help us understand some characteristics of our samples in a more nuanced way. In some support for the economic migration hypothesis for our sample at least, the majority of our interviewees reported that they migrated with their husbands—72 per cent in Dehradun, 78 per cent in Delhi and 70 per cent in Tamil Nadu. Moreover, in Tamil Nadu 26 per cent reported migrating with contractors;

but this was not reported by any interviewees in the other two sites. Others reported migrating with their parents—23 per cent in Dehradun and 7 per cent in Delhi. Moreover, the reality of the agricultural and wage labour situation in the home areas of our sample indicates that many women were already active in earning incomes before their migration—and in that sense these interviews can tell us the manner in which migration affects those in such conditions. And it is particularly striking that the result is to lead us to strongly question the 'received wisdom' that migration improves the living and economic standards of migrants and their families, in any meaningful sense.

Conditions of Work

As our first step towards examining these questions, we look at the conditions that women migrants experience in their sites of employment—in other words, that they face *as workers*.[4]

Wages and Debt

In all areas, and as was the case with men, wages were extremely low. In Delhi, women in construction work reported a wage that was uniformly less than Rs. 300 a day (most reported a wage of Rs. 270, since women are uniformly regarded as 'unskilled' workers in construction), and given the unreliability of construction work this worked out to a monthly income of approximately Rs. 5,000-6,000. Domestic workers in Delhi reported wages ranging from a minimum of Rs. 1,200 per month (1 person or 1 per cent of the sample) to a maximum of Rs. 7,000-8,000 per month (varying with the number of houses; but only one person reported this level of wage as well). The majority of domestic workers reported a wage between Rs. 3,000-Rs. 6,000 per month. In Dehradun, where our sample almost entirely consisted of domestic workers, reported wages were even lower, with 15 per cent of the sample reporting a monthly income of Rs. 1,000 or less, and the majority (47 per cent of the sample) reporting an income of between Rs. 3,000 to Rs. 4,000. In Tamil Nadu, finally, those in construction reported a higher wage than Delhi of Rs. 350-400 a day, which still however works out to approximately Rs. 8,000 a month at most, while those in other occupations reported wages between Rs. 200 to Rs. 300 a day (with, however, a higher frequency of work than in construction, so working out to approximately the same total income).

As we noted in our 2017 study, as per minimum wage regulations, an unskilled worker in the construction sector who works for 25 days per month should receive Rs. 8,075 in Tamil Nadu, Rs. 3,750 in Uttarakhand and Rs. 12,825 in Delhi respectively. These laws, needless to say, do not provide any exception for gender, and this puts the entirety of our sample below or just barely at the minimum wage in all three sites. The male daily wage workers in our sample last year reported incomes that were significantly higher—with 48 per cent of those in Delhi reporting incomes between Rs. 7,000 to Rs. 10,000 a month, and 37 per cent and 49 per cent of those in Dehradun and Tamil Nadu reporting incomes between Rs. 5,000 and Rs. 7,000 a month. But these are still very low absolute incomes, and given that most households in our sample had only two earning members (82 per cent of those in Delhi, 85 per cent in Dehradun and 84 per cent of those in Tamil Nadu), this adds up to family incomes that are well below a living wage.

These wages also come with severe and exploitative conditions of work. As discussed below, construction workers, and especially women construction workers, almost uniformly do not enjoy any of the benefits or safety protections they are entitled to by law. Similarly, domestic workers in our sample often worked difficult hours, especially in Delhi, where two-thirds of the domestic workers worked in three houses or more. In Dehradun this proportion was lower—32 per cent—but 42 per cent reported working in two houses.

Moreover, security of income and employment is essentially non-existent. Fifty-four per cent of those interviewed in Delhi, 22 per cent of those in Dehradun and 20 per cent of those in Tamil Nadu reported routinely receiving their payments late. Eighty-two per cent of those interviewed in Tamil Nadu and 12 per cent in Delhi and Dehradun said that, when payments were late, delays were typically more than a week but less than two weeks. But 12 per cent of those in Delhi reported delays of more than a month. On top of this are the indignities and violations of labour rights discussed in the next section.[5]

Finally, debt levels reflect the extremely low wages being paid. Seventy-five per cent of those in Delhi, 88 per cent in Dehradun and 74 per cent in Tamil Nadu reported that they have to take loans. The single most common reason for doing so was health problems—60 per cent of those in Delhi, 51 per cent in Tamil Nadu and 78 per cent of those in Dehradun cited this as the primary reason for doing so. Reflecting the poverty of these households, the next biggest reason cited was daily expenses—20 per cent in Tamil Nadu and 50 per cent of those in Dehradun mentioned this (only 5 per cent of interviewees mentioned this in Delhi, but that outlier seems more likely to be a survey artifact than a genuine figure). These loans were taken from family and friends in Delhi and Dehradun—roughly 60 per cent in both cases cited this as their primary source of loans—but in Tamil Nadu, perhaps reflecting the greater isolation of these workers, the biggest sources of loans were moneylenders (44 per cent) and contractors (15 per cent). Banks and institutional sources of credit were, needless to say, almost never mentioned—from our entire sample, only four workers in Dehradun mentioned taking loans from banks.

Working Conditions and Labour Rights

Large proportions of our samples reported violations of all basic labour rights. We noted above that payments are often delayed. In addition, 64 per cent of those interviewed in Delhi and 72 per cent of those interviewed in Dehradun said they were asked to do work above and outside their jobs, and 82 per cent and 88 per cent respectively said they were not paid extra for this additional work (the proportion of those reporting such extra work was much smaller in Tamil Nadu—only 6 per cent—a point we return to when discussing the distinct features of our Tamil Nadu sample below). Similarly, 72 per cent of those in Delhi, 59 per cent of those in Dehradun and 96 per cent of those in Tamil Nadu said that if they are late for work, they are insulted and abused.

This situation reflects the state of labour law, or rather the lack of labour law, insofar as casual and unorganised sector labour is concerned in India. Our 2017 study discusses this issue in greater detail, and readers are requested to consult it for a more detailed discussion of each of the applicable laws. Here, we note that the primary applicable laws to this kind of work, where any law applies at all, are the Inter-State Migrant Workers (Regulation of Employment and Conditions of Service) Act, 1979; the Contract Labour (Regulation and Abolition) Act, 1971; and the Building and Other Construction Workers (Regulation of Employment and Conditions of Service) Act, 1996. All these laws provide, on paper, for certain basic rights for workers. These include making non-payment or delayed payment of wages a criminal offence; holding the 'principal employer' (or ultimate beneficiary of the work) liable for wage payments and working conditions; and mandating certain minimum working conditions for all workers covered under them. These minimum working conditions include some points that are of particular importance for women, including toilets and creches for working mothers.

Of course in practice there is probably not a single casual labour work site in India that today provides all (or any) of these facilities, and legal provisions regarding wages are also, as we noted above, essentially never enforced. There are three critical flaws built into the structure of Indian labour law in general, and these laws in particular, that make them unenforceable:[6]

- *Exclusions and Exceptions*: All labour laws of this kind include conditions and numerical limits that exclude the vast majority of workers from their protection. Thus the ISMW Act only applies to workers hired by contractors in one state for work in another state, a condition that would only be true for a very small minority of workers (in Uttarakhand, no establishments, no contractors and no workers had been registered under this Act as of 2012). Both the Contract Labour Act and the Building Workers' Act only apply to work sites of more than

20 and more than ten workers respectively. The single biggest exception, of course, is domestic work, which is not covered by any law at all; India has not ratified the applicable instrument of international law (the ILO Convention on Domestic Work) either. The Minimum Wages Act also simply excludes many sectors, including domestic work.

- *Bars on Filing Complaints:* All Indian labour laws make it impossible for the affected workers to directly file a complaint for violation of the law. The Contract Labour and ISMW Acts require that any complaint must be filed by a Labour Inspector, while the Building Workers' Act liberalises this requirement slightly by allowing complaints to be filed by registered construction workers' unions. For women, this means that in addition to knowing and understanding the law, they then will have to convince a government or union official—who will almost certainly be a man—to file the complaint on their behalf.
- *Burden of Proof*: As we noted last year, though on paper labour laws frequently impose a burden of proof on employers or contractors (for instance, maintenance of muster rolls and ledgers of wage payments is the responsibility of the employer, not of the worker), in practice these laws impose an impossible burden on workers. These workers must first establish that they are covered by the law in the first place; then convince someone else to file a complaint; and then, legal provisions notwithstanding, most authorities demand that workers produce written proof of agreements that are invariably oral.

On top of these fundamental problems are the essential anti-worker bias of the state machinery, the complete absence of provisions intended to address the rights of workers who frequently change employers, and the manner in which state power is deployed—often illegally—to support employers. This means that even the "general" labour laws that are meant to apply to all workers—such as the Workmens' Compensation Act—are also not enforced.

All these problems essentially mean that the vast majority of casual, daily wage and unorganised sector workers in India—of all genders—are effectively unprotected by the law. If these problems apply to men, we can imagine the situation for women. One example illustrates how horrific the situation is. The simple absence of toilets was one crucial point that many of the women in our survey mentioned (and this includes domestic workers, who are often not permitted to use their employers' toilets). This breach of basic law leads to a range of discomfort and health problems that are essentially unimaginable for men—but that affect women literally every day.[7]

2

Access to Welfare Entitlements and Civic Rights

The dire legal situation around workers' rights is then repeated when it comes to access to welfare entitlements. There are two key areas of welfare entitlements that apply to essentially all Indians—access to the public distribution system (the 'ration' system) and healthcare facilities and schemes. We review these here.[8] We also examine voter ID cards and Aadhaar cards, the two other forms of identification and civic rights.

Access to the Public Distribution System

Our findings around access to the ration system in this study paralleled our findings in our previous study on male workers. Seventy-one per cent of those interviewed in Tamil Nadu, 66 per cent in Delhi and 65 per cent of those interviewed in Dehradun reported that they had ration cards. But out of these, 82 per cent in Delhi and all those interviewed in Tamil Nadu had ration cards from their home area—not from their site of work. Dehradun reported a different figure—the vast majority had local ration cards, a point we return to below—but even here only 58 per cent of those interviewed were able to access the PDS.

Inability to access ration supplies, as discussed last year, is not merely a question of being denied some cheaper items. Traders and others aware of the intense vulnerability of migrant workers will often hike prices and cartelise their sales in slums in order to extract more money (knowing their customers cannot go to ration shops). Similarly, states provide not only rations but a range of other welfare benefits through the PDS, especially in states like Tamil Nadu. Exclusion from the PDS thus means simultaneously depriving workers of entitlements and potentially subjecting them to even greater vulnerability.

Healthcare

Practically all our interviewees reported health issues arising from their work—88 per cent of those in Delhi and all those in Dehradun and Tamil Nadu reported health problems. The most common problem reported was body pain in Delhi and Tamil Nadu (75 per cent and 60 per cent respectively) and fevers in Dehradun (66 per cent). This is hardly surprising, considering the exploitative, backbreaking and low paid nature of the work that most of these workers do.

The Rashtriya Swasth Bima Yojana, the predecessor to the newly launched Ayushman Bharat scheme, was supposed to automatically cover several categories of unorganised sector workers that would include our interviewees—including construction workers and domestic workers. Under the scheme, these workers should be issued with "smart cards" that entitle them to up to Rs. 30,000 of health and hospitalisation assistance in a year (the new scheme has raised this upper limit).

But in our interviews, no one in Dehradun and Tamil Nadu reported any assistance from government agencies, and from the entire sample only 15 per cent in Delhi reported receiving assistance from government schemes. Indeed, other than first aid and emergency assistance from employers in case of accidents, none of our interviewees reported receiving any assistance with healthcare expenses at all (other than in the form of taking loans from relatives and friends, as noted above).

Civic Rights

The situation around voter ID cards and Aadhaar cards was better, in some senses, than that around welfare entitlements. Ninety-three per cent of those interviewed in Dehradun, 80 per cent in Delhi and 71 per cent of those interviewed in Tamil Nadu had voter ID cards. However, this did not imply they could exercise their rights locally, since once again a significant proportion of those interviewed—22 per cent in Dehradun, 64 per cent in Delhi and all in Tamil Nadu—reported that their voter ID was for their home area and not for their site of destination. This once again meant that most of our interviewees would not be able to vote in local elections and would have to return to their home area if they wished to do so.

There is a certain irony to the fact that the form of government registration with the highest penetration was the Aadhaar card (as was the case with male workers). All our interviewees in Dehradun, 85 per cent in Delhi and 69 per cent of those in Tamil Nadu reported that they had Aadhaar cards. The irony here is that, other than entitling the user to be subjected to state surveillance, this form of registration (or, more accurately, state *recognition*) conveys no other benefits of its own accord. In this sense the form of state recognition that has reached the most people is also the one that is, in itself, the most useless for them.

3

Discrimination, Harassment and Violence

Migrant workers do not face exploitation merely as workers and as members of the urban poor. They also face specific forms of violence as a result of being *migrants*, and this is particularly pronounced in the case of women.

Discrimination in Housing

In our survey of male workers in 2017 we found that a large proportion—71 per cent, 41 per cent and 30 per cent in Tamil Nadu, Delhi and Dehradun respectively—reported difficulty in finding housing because they were migrants. An even higher proportion—86 per cent in Tamil Nadu, 44 per cent in Delhi and 21 per cent in Dehradun—reported that they had to pay more than locals in order to obtain the same housing. In 2018 we did not repeat this line of questioning, since it seemed that it would not provide much in the way of additional useful data. However, as part of our survey we asked about living conditions, and our findings once again confirmed the extremely poor housing conditions that migrant workers face—as a result not only of their extreme poverty, but as a result of being ghettoised into slums as a result of being migrants.

The majority of our interviewees reported living on rent—all except two who replied in Delhi, half of those interviewed in Dehradun, and 32 per cent in Tamil Nadu. Out of all of our interviewees, only 2 per cent in Delhi and 15 per cent in Dehradun had houses with ownership titles. Those in Tamil Nadu who were not in rented accommodation lived in houses provided by tea estates or factories, or, in the case of 14 per cent of the interviewees, under plastic sheets or other makeshift shelters outside.

Whatever their form of accommodation, a significant proportion had only a single room—68 per cent in Dehradun, 76 per cent in Delhi and 46 per cent in Tamil Nadu. Out of those who had only a single room, more than 90 per cent in Delhi and Dehradun had more than three people staying in that room and more than 50 per cent in both cities had more than five people staying in it. In Tamil Nadu, the proportion was lower, with three quarters of the one room houses having three to four people in them (this is most likely the result of our sample including workers who were housed in estate and factory housing, which generally has two rooms).

As noted in our previous study, these figures, bad as they are, do not capture the full picture. State agencies typically make no effort to extend basic sanitation or other facilities to slums, often on the plea that they are 'illegal' (a consideration that does not seem to apply in the case of wealthy colonies constructed or expanded in violation of the law). In practice the sense that their inhabitants are migrants is taken as a legitimation for this kind of discrimination, a point that we return to below. Meanwhile, as discussed in the previous study, migrant workers face a double whammy in the slums they are forced to live in—since the slums are 'illegal' they are the target of frequent "anti-encroachment" drives, and the rents in these slums are, in proportion to what is actually provided, in fact higher than in other areas.

Insults, Harassment and Violence

The specific, open forms of discrimination such as insults and harassment were reported in Delhi and Tamil Nadu, but Dehradun was an outlier—a point we return to with discussion on our samples in the last section. In Delhi and Tamil Nadu our interviewees widely reported insults for not being "local"—60 per cent in Delhi and 76 per cent in Tamil Nadu reported this. These figures broadly match and tally with those reported by our male respondents in the previous year's survey. Moreover, 37 per cent of those in Delhi and 79 per cent of those interviewed in Tamil Nadu reported feeling unsafe in their area of work. This is in marked contrast to the men interviewed in these locations, who reported much higher levels of feeling 'safe' than women did.

Other forms of harassment were also widely reported, including in Dehradun. Sixty-seven per cent of those interviewed in Dehradun, 53 per cent in Delhi and 78 per cent in Tamil Nadu reported that they felt disrespected at work, including through the use of threats and insults. Moreover, 14 per cent of those interviewed in Delhi and 12 per cent in Tamil Nadu reported they had faced physical violence.

In addition to these forms of harassment, we also specifically asked about any form of 'untouchability', including in the provision of water and food. Interestingly, our Tamil Nadu interviewees did not report any such untouchability (though this perhaps may also be related to the fact that none of those workers worked within homes). In Delhi a full 40 per cent of those interviewed reported facing such forms of untouchability, in particular through being forced to use separate water glasses. In Dehradun, only 5 per cent of those interviewed reported feeling like they faced untouchability, in the form of separate food and water.

While our survey included a question about sexual harassment, given that, as discussed in the methodology section, we did not interview women in private settings, it is perhaps not surprising that most did not report such harassment to be occurring. However, even with this poor context and with great reluctance, 14 per cent of those interviewed in Tamil Nadu reported that they had also faced sexual harassment while working.

Discrimination by Police and State Agencies

In addition to discrimination from employers and others, migrant workers also face severe discrimination from the police. Our interviewees reported facing suspicion and harassment from the police—indeed this was almost uniformly reported in Tamil Nadu, with 25 per cent in Delhi reporting the same. Continuing with the pattern of being an outlier, none of the interviewees in Dehradun reported problems from the police. Almost none of our interviewees, with the exception of a handful in Delhi, reported facing false cases or physical violence from the police (three and four workers, respectively, reported such incidents in Delhi). This was in contrast to male migrant workers in our 2017 study, who had reported such incidents at a much higher frequency, with a full 70 per cent in Tamil Nadu reporting facing false cases and 21 per cent reported being beaten.

Moreover, as reported in last year's study, police violence against migrants brings other dimensions beyond the violence itself. The police frequently refuse to protect migrants or to investigate and prosecute crimes against them. The usual protections that are invoked by the poor against police atrocities—connections to political leaders, caste and other solidarity networks—are also much less available to migrant workers, and especially to migrant women.

Finally, as is the case with men, women migrant workers also face discrimination at the hands of other state agencies. These include, as we noted above, the Labour Department, which simply does not enforce laws meant to protect workers (even in the rare cases where such laws apply). In our 2017 study, we interviewed officials in the Labour Departments of Delhi and Dehradun, who both asserted that they had neither the staff nor the interest to implement laws for migrant workers (beyond welfare schemes). In Tamil Nadu, we noted, "the workers we interviewed had never seen nor heard of the Labour Department or its role—either as enforcer of the law or as provider of welfare."

Similarly, as we noted in last year's study, the municipal corporations of Delhi and Dehradun and the revenue departments of these states do not allocate land or housing where these workers can live. Even courts are guilty of much the same approach. For instance, in the discussion seminar on this study that was held on November 1, 2018, the women workers present stressed how the Supreme Court's ban on construction activities in the days preceding Diwali—in order to reduce air pollution—had been passed and implemented without any regard for the tremendous blow this was to the wages and incomes of daily wage workers who depend on such work. To the extent that we are aware, this issue was not even raised in court.

As with men, women migrant workers thus face a situation where state agencies essentially act as if they do not exist—and refuse to implement either laws or welfare schemes in their favour.

4

Intersections Between Patriarchy, Migration, Caste and Class

Our study also sought to examine the experience of migration itself, within the context of the multiple oppressions of caste, class, community and gender that migrant women workers face. What we found in this respect does not fully confirm common notions about the effects and 'benefits' of migration. The usual consensus on migration is that it weakens some forms of caste oppression—rigid caste bonds—and some forms of patriarchal oppression, particularly around movement and public activity (see, for instance, the discussions in Shanthi (2006) and Srinivasan (1997)). This is also the public policy common sense. Our data did not show any unequivocal trend in this direction, however. Instead it showed a considerably more complex picture.

We note, for instance, that—as discussed above—the 'big' city of Delhi showed a high share of workers (40 per cent) reporting some form of untouchability being practised against them. Similarly, insofar as patriarchal bonds are concerned, our interviewees reported very high rates of domestic violence (despite, as noted above, the fact that the interviews were not conducted in private settings). Fifty-six per cent of those interviewed in Delhi, 23 per cent of those interviewed in Dehradun and 46 per cent of those interviewed in Tamil Nadu reported experiencing domestic violence at home, with husbands being the most common perpetrators (in-laws being the second most common). In all three sites interviewees repeatedly mentioned alcoholism as a common problem and a reason for domestic violence.

When it comes to shifts in family relationships—especially between husband and wife—our data showed a positive pattern, but not a strong one. In Dehradun and Tamil Nadu, a slightly higher proportion of women reported that their husbands helped with housework after migration. There was an increase of six percentage points in the case of Tamil Nadu, 15 percentage points in the case of Dehradun and 19 percentage points in the case of Delhi (indeed, in Delhi, only 9 per cent of women reported that their husbands helped with housework before migration, while 28 per cent reported that they did so after migration). When asked about domestic housework in general, the majority of the interviewees in all three sites felt that their domestic workload had lessened after migration (89 per cent in Tamil Nadu, 55 per cent in Dehradun and 57 per cent in Delhi). All of this does indicate a certain weakening of patriarchal bonds within the household, but it does not show a radical transformation. Perhaps most indicative of this is the continuing prevalence of very high rates of domestic violence and the fact that the sharing of housework, even in the smaller and more independent households that follow migration into urban areas, does not change to a major level.

Our survey also included general questions on safety, as noted earlier, and on whether or not our interviewees felt more free to move around. To the latter question, 60 per cent of those in Delhi and 98 per cent of those interviewed in Dehradun felt freer in moving around in their site of destination—but this was reversed in Tamil Nadu, where 84 per cent reported that they felt more free to move around in their home areas. Both the answers to the question on a general feeling of 'safety' and the answer to this question indicate that migration, and migration to urban areas in particular, *may* weaken the hold of wider structures of social oppression on women—but also may not do so, as occurred in Tamil Nadu.

It should be noted that these points barely scratch the surface of the shifts in domestic and social patriarchal structures that occur alongside migration. This is an area where survey based and comparative research like ours cannot achieve an in-depth analysis—and need to be complemented by ethnographic and in-depth studies that look at these questions in greater depth and particularity.

However, overall, our data did allow to identify three overall trends that particularly require discussion. The first was the extreme and intense exploitation of our interviewees as *workers*. The second, as noted above, was the prevalence of untouchability and discrimination on both migrant and, implicitly, caste grounds in Delhi and Tamil Nadu (though with a much lower prevalence in Dehradun—this difference is discussed in the next section). The high figure for untouchability in Delhi is particularly notable here. The third is the particular changes in domestic and social patriarchal structures that accompanied migration—and we noted that these are relatively small, and also not uniformly positive.

Overall, these three trends indicate a kind of *nexus of superexploitation* with these women at its centre. What we might broadly call three axes of oppression—class, caste/community, and patriarchy—overlap and reinforce one another, each acting separately and jointly to disempower these women and to undercut their humanity.[9] The result is a situation that is both *brutal* and *inhuman* and which should have no place in any society.

The relevant question for us, and indeed for any study of these issues, cannot and should not be whether this situation is "better" or "worse" than the situation that women experienced before migration. This question is both an insult to the dignity of the people in question and a sterile proposition—supposing it is indeed "better", does that mean policy or political action should promote this kind of situation? The real issue is whether and in what manner this nexus can be weakened and fought against, wherever it occurs. We return to this approach in the Conclusion.

5

Differences and Parallels in Our Study Sites

For most of this paper we have examined the parallels and commonalities in the responses of our interviewees across our study sites. But there are, as has been noted, marked differences both in the nature of the sample groups in each site, as well as in how they responded.

Broadly speaking, these differences are on two lines. The first is the differences that are dictated by the overall context in which these workers live and work—namely the contexts of Uttarakhand, Delhi and Tamil Nadu. Here we note some of the salient differences in these sites. Readers who are interested in a more detailed discussion can also consult our 2017 study.

In terms of the overall political atmosphere that migrants experience, Tamil Nadu is clearly an outlier among these three states in terms of the isolation and discrimination that migrants experience. The language barrier is perhaps the most fundamental problem (though it is notable that a third of our respondents reported that they had learned Tamil, in contrast to their male counterparts, almost none of whom had managed to learn the language). In addition, chauvinistic mobilisation by Tamil political parties and social movements has repeatedly targeted migrants—referred to, derisively, as "north Indians"—and they have also repeatedly faced police brutality and state "verification" campaigns (see Dutta (2012) and Warrier (2012)). All of this doubly impacts women, and hence it is not surprising that they reported both high levels of feeling 'unsafe' and a sense of not being able to move as freely in Tamil Nadu as in their home areas.

Uttarakhand has experienced less vocal and open anti-migrant campaigns, but since the time of the statehood campaign, anti-migrant sentiment has been common among both the general population and among political organisations in the state (a sentiment reflected, as we noted last year, in statements by Labour Department officials that they "are not responsible for these outsiders" who should be "taken care of by their own governments"). Though migrants experience a language barrier in Uttarakhand as well—since migrants frequently speak languages such as Maithili, Maghadi or Bhojpuri rather than Hindi—the relative closeness of these languages to Hindi reduces linguistic and physical isolation. Further, as we discuss below, the nature of our sample in Dehradun offered us an insight into a different type of population than our interviewees in Delhi and Tamil Nadu.

Delhi has perhaps the least openly anti-migrant atmosphere of these three states, but given the context, this is not saying much. Anti-migrant sentiment targeting working class migrants is common in Delhi as well, and Labour Department officials washing their hands of the rights of migrant workers is extremely common in Delhi as well. Delhi also resembles Tamil Nadu in the common practice of equating migrant workers with criminals—though, as we noted above, this appears to less directly affect women workers than it does men (in terms of police violence and cases).

In our study these differences in context then are refracted through, and have to be seen in light of, the differences in the character of our samples. Here we can place our three study sites on a kind of spectrum. Our interviewees in Dehradun represented, in some senses, a stable and older population. Fifty-eight per cent had been working in the city for more than 15 years (86 per cent for more than 3 years), 96 per cent had children who lived with them, and practically all were employed in domestic work that paid on a monthly basis. At the opposite extreme is our sample in Tamil Nadu, 79 per cent of whom had been in their present location for less than two years (24 per cent for less than six months), 36 per cent of whom either did not have children or whose children were not living with them, and all of whom were on daily wages. Given their short periods of stay, our Tamil Nadu sample also represented migrants who return to their home areas much more frequently than those in our other two sites (and in that sense may be regarded as "seasonal" migrants[10] Our Delhi sample fell between these samples, with the majority (70 per cent) having worked in their present location for between two and five years.

Given the combination between the character of our samples and the overall context, we should note that in a sense our

Dehradun interviewees represented the positive extreme of the continuum between higher and lower security, and our Tamil Nadu interviewees represented the opposite extreme. What impact did these differences have? As we noted last year, when our samples had similar characteristics, it is striking how *small* the impact actually appears to be. As we mentioned above, all our interviewees reported facing brutal oppression on multiple counts, reflecting how hard it is for a working class migrant in India to ever *not* face discrimination and exploitation—however long they may live in any one location.

In the specific case of women migrant workers, we can break this conclusion down further along the three axes of oppression discussed in the previous section—caste/community, gender and class. Broadly, from our data, it appears that only the first axis—and to a limited extent—show significant differences as a result of the differences in our sites of study. Our interviewees in Dehradun faced relatively lower levels of open insults or police violence. As a knock on effect, their ability to move more freely was higher, which arguably affects patriarchal oppression as well. But nevertheless, the overall functioning of the system that oppressed women was not massively affected by these differences.

Indeed, on the question of class oppression, it was striking that women who had remained in Dehradun for many years had been unable to move into more secure or less exploitative forms of work than domestic work.[11] This is in contrast to male migrant workers, who, as we observed in our previous study, had a tendency to move, over time, from less stable to more stable, and from less skilled to more skilled, forms of work the longer they remained in one place.

This overall finding reinforces what we noted in the previous section. It is particularly useful in the light of frequent policy and social prescriptions that advocate migration as some kind of panacea for various forms of oppression and poverty, and particularly for oppression of women. If migration into relatively more 'secure' occupations, for far longer periods of time, in states that are relatively less 'anti-migrant', *still* makes a marginal difference to the kind of exploitation people face, such claims are mistaken at best and deliberately dishonest at worst. Structures of exploitation need to be confronted and challenged, not indirectly reinforced by policies and arguments that elide them.

6

Ways Forward

The findings of our study demonstrate that achieving higher standards of living, greater freedom and greater dignity for working class migrant women workers cannot merely be a question of welfare policies. Indeed, the existing welfare policies are barely implemented, and even if they were implemented, would not—on their own—address the fundamental problems that these workers face. Hence, as in our 2017 study, we understand the essential problem to be *political* in character, in the sense of revolving around the ability of workers to confront the power structures that oppress them. We hold that both policies and political action hence must be directed towards this end rather than towards generic 'welfare' improvements.[12]

In light of this approach, we return to the three axes of oppression discussed above. Each of these axes has its own specific, particular features that need to be confronted.

- *Class Oppression*: Daily wage workers, whatever their gender, face a particular set of constraints on their ability to confront their exploitation as workers. These constraints include the impermanent and casual nature of their work; the utter lack of security of employment; the competition between individual workers; the lack of meaningful legal protection in the workplace, with accompanying harassment and violence; and the layers of subcontracting that frequently lie between workers and their employers, atomising the workforce and making struggle more difficult. These constraints apply with even more force to the types of work that women workers undertake. Domestic workers face them in an extreme fashion, since in most cases they work alone and sometimes—in the case of so-called "live in" workers—on a 14 hour, seven-day basis, with minimal contact with anyone other than their employers. Women workers in construction are almost uniformly regarded as "unskilled" and occupy the lowest position in the construction labour hierarchy, making them even more vulnerable.

- *Caste and Community Oppression*: This is of course not actually one axis of oppression, but a cluster of related structures around caste, status as migrants, religion, ethnicity, etc. For the purposes of our discussion in this paper we refer to these structures together as they have certain shared characteristics. They all manifest in the form of verbal harassment, physical violence and physical and social isolation. These constraints apply to all genders, but once again there are particular features of such forms of oppression that affect women more. Poor housing and public facilities, with their accompanying childcare and health implications, have a far greater impact on women than on men. Caste harassment and violence also often has a gendered quality.

- *Patriarchal Oppression*: Finally, and perhaps most of all, oppression of women *qua* women is intense and often brutal in the case of migrant women workers. This manifests in four related spaces—the workplace, public spaces, state agencies and the home. In the case of the workplace, sexual harassment is an ever present threat, as is gender discrimination in wages and types of work. In public spaces, freedom of movement is impeded both by domestic restrictions and by fear of physical danger—as we saw in the case of Tamil Nadu. State agencies, being overwhelmingly male, are dangerous and insensitive spaces—and as a result for most migrant women workers they are basically inaccessible and are never approached alone. Finally, in the home, migrant women workers face, as we saw, a high level of domestic violence, a high workload (notwithstanding the slightly higher degree to which men contribute after migration), non-existent childcare facilities, and the problems that come with health crises, poor schooling and lack of physical safety for either children or themselves. They also confront widespread alcoholism.

All these factors contribute to a prevalence of *atomisation*, *cynicism* and *despair* among migrant workers—which then, in the case of women, is compounded by a much higher sense of *fear* than their male counterparts experience. These obstacles in turn present a key challenge to collective action. As a result, most political activity among migrant workers (men and women) consists of short-term, transactional patron-client relations between the workers and more powerful 'leaders'—who promise security, protection from eviction, or just plain cash in exchange for support. This political demobilisation, perhaps more so than among almost any other segment of Indian society, is what enables the extreme oppression of migrant workers that we discussed here.

But political demobilisation is only one side of the coin. The other side is the role of the state—both as a cause and as an effect of this demobilisation. In all three axes of oppression, the state machinery acts in a manner that is both apparent and crucial. It is the state, through its legal chicanery and non-enforcement of applicable laws, that connives with and encourages the kind of extraordinary class exploitation that these workers face. It is the state, through its non-implementation of housing schemes and other forms of public provision, combined with its complete partiality towards upper caste, local Hindu men, that does the same for caste and community oppression. Finally, the state's role in enabling and promoting patriarchy is so obvious it does not even need discussion. Without state connivance, the political regime that migrant workers face would be far weaker—and their collective strength far stronger.

In this sense, the priority for both policy and political action must be to confront not just one employer or one site of exploitation, but the failure and connivance of the state. As argued in our 2017 study, the key issue here is the manner in which migrant workers are systematically *disorganised*—by a lack of recognition and a lack of security. These issues, rather than those of welfare alone, need to be the target of organising and political action in the case of women workers as well. Moreover, steps on these lines need to explicitly target patriarchal norms as well.

In the remainder of this paper, we outline some initial steps that can be taken in this direction.

Steps for Policy and Organised Action

In our 2017 study, we noted that the crucial role of the state in disorganising workers means that some of the most effective, and most radical, steps can be those that seek to alter state action. Of course, merely asking the state to act—whether that means asking it to implement labour law, or to implement welfare schemes—can be a dead end. However, if such struggles are specifically aimed at not only gaining specific *benefits*, but at addressing the manner in which the state machinery atomises and disempowers workers, they can be powerful steps towards change.

For men, as we noted in 2017, the fundamental problems of *recognition*, *inclusion* and *security* make organising and defending one's rights extremely difficult. In the case of women, we need to add patriarchal oppression—with its combination of domestic and external control—to this list. In this sense, forms of organising that defeat the first three problems are necessary, but with an additional axis that also seeks to specifically address oppression of women *qua* women.

A burgeoning wave of domestic workers' movements in India has raised a number of demands that in some ways fit into this broader framework. These include:

- A separate law for domestic workers that recognises elementary labour rights such as working hours, paid leave and protections in case of harassment and non-payment of wages.

- Provisions in such a law for an effective regulatory machinery—not the deliberate sabotage that is embedded into existing laws (as discussed above).
- Healthcare and social security provisions for domestic workers.

These demands offer a start, but they are limited to domestic workers. But the same principles can be extended to other policies or demands. For instance, some possibilities include:

- Demanding or instituting a registration drive for women migrant workers in order to enable access to healthcare—both through existing health insurance schemes and through the public healthcare system. Such a demand would not only possibly improve health services, it would also provide a form of state recognition that would be useful.
- The combination of poor healthcare, poor schooling and non-existent childcare results in migrant women—and poor women in general—having extremely limited time outside housework and paid work. This impedes both their lives in general and their ability to struggle for their rights. Given this, while general struggles by migrant workers for greater security—such as for slum regularisation and an end to police violence—can improve both the immediate situation and the prospects for political organising, specific demands for creches, government schools, and for the effective implementation of the Integrated Child Development Scheme (ICDS)

among the urban poor can enhance the prospects of such struggles for women workers.[13]

- Coming from the other direction, so to speak, movements that seek to tackle patriarchal oppression—such as those against domestic violence, for a more gender just police force, etc.—can also benefit from taking into account the specific forms of oppression that migrant women encounter. These can include asking for separate surveys and registration drives that address the problems of women who are not settled in one location, and for steps to tackle domestic and public violence against such women.
- All of this in addition to the general movements for migrant workers' rights, and policy steps to address the sabotage of labour law, that we discussed in our previous study. These include easier registration, enabling workers to file police complaints for violations, etc. In this context, one particular step deserves special mention—many states have "right to service" laws (with varying degrees of success in enforcement), but it is striking that rights legislations and welfare schemes for workers are almost never included in these laws. Fighting for this inclusion is a small step that initiates a process by which officials can be held accountable for failures in implementation. This would ideally lead up to a struggle for the larger changes in labour law that are required, such as removing the restrictions for filing of complaints, providing civil and criminal liability for officials who do not carry out their duties, and so on.

While unions and other forms of mass struggle can raise these issues, autonomous organising among women workers also occurs in any case. Specifically attempting to enable such organising, such as by, for instance, organising women-only slum meetings, separate women's wings in workers' organisations, etc., can also help address the superexploitation of these workers.

We are not providing a more specific prescription here as the specific steps to be taken to target these issues depends on state-specific and politically contingent constraints—the same measure (for instance, better registration of construction workers) will have a very different meaning in different states and at different times. However, we hope that these general principles may help to provide a framework for analysing what will be most effective in each situation.

We note, in conclusion, that many would dismiss the above as "reformist" or "welfarist" measures. As we argued in our previous study, such analyses are misleading. When the structures (or, more accurately, the *process*) of state functioning and of political power are precisely what enables the superexploitation of women workers, framing more 'traditional' demands for either political power or collective bargaining are unlikely to result in either mass political action or in any significant changes. Struggles need to target the actual processes that, we repeat, *disorganise* workers—and it is only through those actions that they can lay the ground for subsequent, deeper shifts towards greater justice.

And such struggles are not only necessary for women migrant workers. In our previous study, we noted that "The extraordinary superexploitation and inhuman oppression of migrant workers constitutes one of the most glaring black marks on the record of the Indian state and ruling classes since independence." This is doubly the case with women migrant workers, who, as we mentioned above, live not only in an environment of extreme inhumanity but also one pervaded with *fear*. Changing this situation is vital to all of Indian society as a whole—for the continued extreme oppression of one class only enables the oppression of all.

Notes

1. In this context, it should be noted that all the researchers for this study are affiliated to workers' organisations and other groups, though these organisations do not endorse and are not in any way connected to this study.

2. As observed by our reviewer Pratyush Chandra in 2017, this should not be seen as a cause of all migration, only of particular forms.

3. See discussions in Shah and Harriss-White (2011) and in Gopalakrishnan and Sreenivasa (2009) for more details.

4. This section consciously follows the same structure as our 2017 study, in order to ease drawing parallels and comparisons.

5. We are indebted to Dr. K.B. Saxena, one of our reviewers, for raising the role of placement agencies in the recruitment and exploitation of domestic workers. These agencies—which appear to be much more prevalent in Delhi—act as a kind of 'super-contractor', taking a major cut out of the wages of workers hired through them and effectively

preventing them from engaging in any kind of organising or struggle for their rights. Unfortunately, given that this study was not specifically focused on domestic workers, we did not investigate this aspect in our field surveys. However, the issue is briefly discussed in Kumar and Chauhan (2014).

6. This point is also discussed further in our 2017 study.
7. We are grateful to the women workers' who attended our discussion seminar on this study for strongly stressing this point.
8. In our 2017 study on male migrant workers, we had also examined the functioning of welfare schemes under Building and Other Construction Workers Act. In this study, we did not examine this issue separately, as only our sample in Delhi included a large number of construction workers.
9. Moreover, these axes of oppression do not exist independently—they also create each other, under the overarching fundamental dynamic of a capitalist society, which reconfigures and reproduces them. A full exploration of this question is out of our scope here, but we are indebted to our reviewer Pratyush Chandra for raising this crucial point.
10. It should be noted that it is difficult to draw a clear line between 'seasonal' migrants and more settled migrants. The transitions between different forms of migration, on the continuum between short-term and long-term forms, is discussed in more detail in our 2017 study. In this study, given this, we did not seek to differentiate these categories, but instead sought to differentiate migrants on the basis of their current period of stay.
11. We are indebted to our reviewers Adv. Seema Misra and Dr. K.B. Saxena for raising this question.

12. Many of the points in this section have been discussed in much greater detail in our 2017 study. In order to avoid repetition, those arguments are presented in a summary form here.

13. For instance, our reviewer Dr. K.B. Saxena pointed out that most cities do not even have allocated spaces for ICDS anganwadis.

References

Bhatt, Wasudha. 2009. "The Gender Dimension of Migration in India: The Politics of Contemporary Space in Orissa and Rajasthan." *Development in Practice* 19 (1). Taylor & Francis Ltd., Oxfam GB: 87–93.

Breman, Jan. 1994. *Wage Hunters and Gatherers*. Oxford University Press.

Dutta, Madhumita. 2012. "Come South, Young Man, But Here Be Dragons." *The Hindu*.

Gopalakrishnan, Shankar, M.S. Selvaraj, Ramendra Kumar, and Trepan Singh Chauhan. 2017. *Conditions of Work and Political Consciousness Among Migrant Workers in Three States*. Aakar Books.

Gopalakrishnan, Shankar, and Priya Sreenivasa. 2009. *The Political Economy of Migration*. New Delhi: Aakar Books.

Kumar, Ramendra, and Trepan Singh Chauhan. 2014. *Domestic Workers in Delhi and Dehradun: Oppression in the Space of the Home*. https://srcindia.wordpress.com/2015/01/domestic_workers_study_dec_2014_final.pdf.

Mazumdar, Indrani. 2013. "Migration and Gender in India." *Economic and Political Weekly* Vol. 48 (Issue No. 10).

National Sample Survey Organisation. 2010. "Migration in India: NSSO 64th Round." Ministry of Statistics and Programme Implementation.

Shah, Alpa, and Barbara Harriss-White. 2011. "Resurrecting Scholarship on Agrarian Transformations." *Economic and Political Weekly* XLVI (39): 13–18.

Shanthi, K. 2006. "Female Labour Migration in India: Insights from NSSO Data." Working Papers. Madras School of Economics.

Srinivasan, Shobha. 1997. "Breaking Rural Bonds Through Migration: The Failure of Development for Women in India." *Journal of Comparative Family Studies* 28 (1): 89–102.

Warrier, Shobha. 2012. "In Tamil Nadu, the Administration Itself Is Targeting People." *Rediff.com.*

Acknowledgements

We are grateful to our research assistants Rajendra Shah, Kamala, L. Priyanka and Sudita for their assistance over the course of the study.

We also owe our gratitude to our reviewers in the discussion seminar held on November 1st—Dr. K.B. Saxena, Pratyush Chandra, Adv. Seema Misra and members and leaders of Delhi Shramik Sanghatan—who provided valuable advice and suggestions for the study. We are above all grateful to the approximately thirty women workers who took time out of their schedules to join us for a seminar to review an earlier draft of this study.

Finally, this study was sponsored by the Rosa Luxemburg Foundation e.V. with funds of the Federal Ministry for Economic Cooperation and Development of the Federal Republic of Germany. The Rosa Luxemburg Stiftung (RLS) is a German-based foundation working in South Asia and other parts of the world on the subjects of critical social analysis and civic education. It promotes a sovereign, socialist, secular, and democratic social order, and aims to present members of society and decision-makers with alternative approaches to such an order. Research organisations, groups working for social emancipation, and social activists are supported in their initiatives to develop models that have the potential to deliver social and economic justice.

The study would not have been possible without this generous support and the assistance of the programme manager at the foundation, Rajiv Kumar, or the South Asia Director of the foundation, Stefan Mentschel.